GERMAN VEHICLES IN WORLD WAR II

Motorcycles of the Wehrmacht

A Photo Chronicle

Horst Hinrichsen

The Allies also painted their war materials used in the southern theaters of war with yellow-brown paint. This model of a Harley-Davidson WLA 45 is painted light tan, the color of sand.

GERMAN VEHICLES IN WORLD WAR II

Motorcycles of the Wehrmacht

A Photo Chronicle

Horst Hinrichsen

Schiffer Military History
Atglen, PA

Translated from the German by Dr. Edward Force.

This book was originally published under the title,
Kräder der Wehrmacht,
by Podzun-Pallas Verlag.

Library of Congress Catalog Number: 94-66974

Printed in the United States of America.
ISBN: 0-88740-685-8

We are interested in hearing from authors with book ideas on related topics.

Published by Schiffer Publishing Ltd.
77 Lower Valley Road
Atglen, PA 19310
Please write for a free catalog.
This book may be purchased from the publisher.
Please include $2.95 postage.
Try your bookstore first.

CONTENTS

The BMW R 75 model in so-called "African paint." In Army Directive 1943, No. 181, it was ordered that large military equipment in all theaters of war be painted a uniform dark yellow.

Foreword

The military motorcycle drivers – or as they were called in the customary slang, the "Kradfahrer" – had a shadowy existence in the structure of the German Army between 1935 and 1945. Of course, when the major military equipment of the time is discussed, there will be a reference here and there to the motorcyclists with their solo and sidecar cycles.

The motorcycle riflemen are an exception. But as combat units, they could be described and portrayed more vividly. On the other hand, photographs of motorcyclists, such as motorcycle messengers, are only found occasionally, like lone flowers in a big meadow. Therefore this book is dedicated to all the motorcycle drivers with their various machines and types of service. Thus it does not matter whether the subject is the tough driver of an off-road heavy motorcycle rifle unit's machine or the draftee with his formerly private, now requisitioned light road cycle. All of them will be portrayed once more in "words and pictures." A long-winded chronological portrayal of all cycles that saw service, with all their technical details, has been avoided deliberately. Sufficient books on that subject have been published already.

Rather, a vivid mixture of action photos is offered, to give the postwar generation insight into the everyday military life of these modern "mounted messengers" and "motorized hussars."

Thus this book contains not only striking combat photos that show the dedicated, forward-moving motorcyclist on his mount. In many privately-owned photos, the comradeship of the motorcyclist is documented in other aspects of everyday military life. For example, there is the small group of motorcycle messengers in their shirt sleeves lurking behind a Russian cottage, their stripped-to-the-waist efforts to repair their cycles in the field, their comradeship, even between superiors and inferiors in service, when it was necessary to get a sidecar cycle out of the mud and on its way again, or just the "quiet" photo to remember the motorcyclist and his cycle by, the cycle painted black with gold trim. Thus was he photographed one last time before he left his parental home. Did he ever return?

To all of them who had to spend their best years "in the saddle", this book is dedicated.

Hamburg, autumn 1993
Horst Hinrichsen

Motorcycles of the Wehrmacht

"The motor bicycle placed at the disposal of InfantryRegiment No. 122 was used during the corps maneuvers for the division staff. Cycles and drivers have proved themselves reliable and capable in every way."

This song of praise to the first "cycle messengers" was written to the Neckarsulm Bicycle Works by the Commander of the 28th Division of the XIIth Army Corps, Duke Albrecht of Württemberg, on September 25, 1904. The use of "steel horses" had commenced its unending course at the beginning of the Kaiser's maneuver's in 1904. Gefreiter Wilhelm Kohler, later Managing Chief Engineer at NSU, was at this time the first motorcyclist in the army of Württemberg.

Father . . .

Gefr. Wilhelm Hokler (born 1881) as a member of the Army of Württemberg, with his 4 HP, one-cylinder NSU motorcycle in 1904. What was then the Neckarsulmer Fahrzeugwerke AG made this motorcycle available on loan to the 28th Division for maneuvers, so that the officers could come to know the value of such a speedy means of carrying messages and commands (and naturally of carrying supplies as well). Until 1934, Mr. K. was the leading chief engineer at the NSU works and thus played a decisive role in the development of this world-renowned motorcycle marque.

Although the picture of the motorcycle messenger has changed considerably from the turn of the century to the present, even today, in the days of medium- and long-range rockets and space surveillance with the most modern radar and electronic satellites, the simple soldiers on their off-road steel steeds are still a means of action that no military commander would want to do without.

In the present-day Bundeswehr as in the former Wehrmacht, the training of motorcycle messengers has taken a particular place. The motorcycle messenger is a lone warrior. A good sense of orientation in unknown country and the ability to read military maps quickly without errors are, along with driving ability, the chief requirements of the motorcycle messenger. Often enough it has been the motorcycle messenger who has been able to deliver an order or a message at the decisive moment, because other means of communication were not available or not functioning. But the motorcycle messenger can also be used for short periods as a scout or a traffic director. Countless combat units, large or small, have reached their place of action by changing positions in the night under the direction of a motorcycle messenger, because he had scouted the appropriate line of march in daylight. The motorcycle riflemen, on the other hand, are quite different. They formed regular combat troops, originally at battalion strength. Used predominantly for reconnaissance, forward, flank, communication, rear-guard and surprise-attack tasks of all kinds, these "hussars of the infantry" won their own renown as the "fastest earthbound weapon" in direct combat.

Though there were only a few thousand motorcycles that saw service in World War I, their numbers rose to the tens of thousands at the beginning of World War II.

. . . and Son

Panzerschütze Hans Kohler, born in 1914, of the 3rd Company, Panzer Regiment 4 in Ohrdruf, Thuringia, on a BMW R 4 in 1936. Panzer Regiment 4 was formed in 1935-36 at the Ohrdrup troop training center and later transferred to Schweinfurt and then Vienna. The present-day Dr. H. Kohler, son of the aforementioned W. Kohler, was also active at the NSU works in the mid-1930s.

With the reintroduction of universal military obligations in 1936 and the preparations for war beginning in 1938, there was already a great need for military motorcycles, which could not be met by the industry in a short time. The result was that, first of all, the motorcycles of various types owned by the private sector were requisitioned for military purposes. The motorcycles delivered by the industry included models by BMW, Zündapp, Victoria, Triumph, NSU and DKW. The number of models of requisitioned motorcycles can no longer be determined today. In fact, even motorcycles captured from the enemy in the early days of the war were repainted and used for German military purposes.

To visualize the variety of models of motorcycles used by the German Army from 1935 on, here is a list that cannot claim to be complete. Many requisitioned motorcycles were not included in official statistics:

BMW R 4	Zündapp DB 200	NSU Pony 100	DKW RT 125
BMW R 12	Zündapp K 500 W	NSU 201 ZDB	DKW NZ 350
BMW R 23	Zündapp KS 600 W	NSU 251 OSL	Triumph BD 250/1
BMW R 35	Zündapp K 800 W	NSU 351 OSL	Triumph S 350
BMW R 75	Zündapp KS 750	NSU 501 OSL	Victoria KR 35 WH
		NSU 601 OSL	Victoria K 6
		NSU 501 TS	
		NSU 601 TS	

In all, motorcycle production in the German Reich added up to 200,000 machines in 1938 alone. As before, these were not special military motorcycles, but those from series production. Their basic equipment included only rough-tread tires, saddlebags and appropriate Wehrmacht paint.

Within the framework of general mobilization, as well as later in the war, all privately owned motorcycles were also requisitioned, repainted, and turned over to the Wehrmacht for use in the war. Trained individuals from the motorcycle industry were called in as so-called "evaluators." Their task consisted of determining the value of the requisitioned motorcycles in Reichsmark, so that the owners who had to surrender a good piece of their property could be compensated. The resulting variety of models brought the motorcycle supplying of the German Army almost to a standstill, for on account of the great variety of models, sufficient spare parts could not be supplied at the right time.

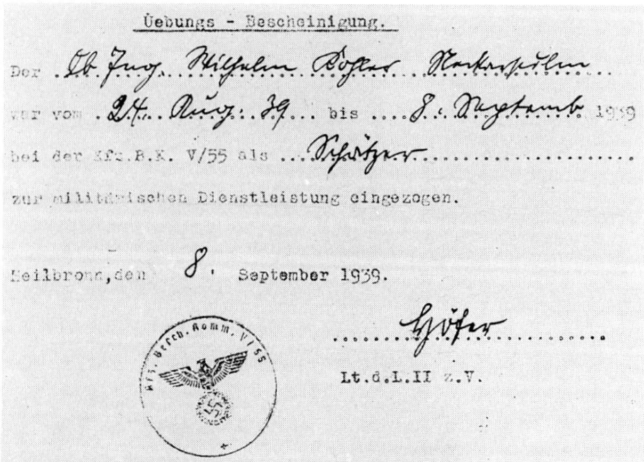
Üebungs - Bescheinigung.

Der Ob. Ing. Wilhelm Kohler Neckarsulm

war vom 24. Aug. 39 bis 8. Septemb. 1939

bei der Kfz.B.K. V/55 als Schätzer

zur militärischen Dienstleistung eingezogen.

Heilbronn, den 8. September 1939.

Höfer

Lt.d.L.II z.V.

In the process of mobilization for World War II, which began on September 1, 1939, all civilian motorcycles were confiscated and used for military purposes. For this purpose, recognized experts from the motorcycle industry were called in as "assessors", whose job it was to evaluate the confiscated motorcycles in Reichsmarks, so that the owners could be compensated. This activity was described as "practice." Often the motorcycle and its owner were called to arms together. In this case, the aforementioned Senior Engineer W. Kohler was called in for this activity. The date of the document is of interest. Obviously, civilian motorcycles were needed even before the outbreak of World War II.

These motorcycles fulfilled their purpose as long as they were used on more or less paved roads or smooth country. For example, the following quotations come from field-post letters written by motorcycle messengers who wrote the following to their former employer, the NSU works, about their experiences in the early years of the war:

"... On September 21 it has been five years since I bought it new at your Stuttgart branch, where I worked as a mechanic since August 1939. Since the end of August I have been in Wehrmacht service with the motorcycle, which I myself have always driven since then. During the four years of my private driving, the machine always functioned to my complete satisfaction, as it has now, since I have been drafted. In this year I have driven it 20,000 km, at first in the polish campaign, then during service in the operational area of the western front and on duty in France. During the campaign in France I drove about 7000 km.... If possible, I want to buy back the machine after the end of the war we have been compelled to wage."

"... All our vehicles, and particularly our NSU machines, have come through the days of marching without the slightest problem, although we have not shown them much mercy. I am proud of the fact that my firm has done so well...."

"... Here I am now in service as a motorcycle messenger. We also had motorcycles in France, and there was also one NSU 251 OSL machine there...."

"... In our free hours we often talk of the quality and reliability of our good NSU motorcycles. A man from Baden said: I have already had three motorcycles, but I have never yet had such a fine machine as my NSU 500...."

"... I am in service here as a radioman and have had the good fortune of taking part in the great victorious procession through Holland, Belgium and Flanders. Today we are just a few kilometers from Paris. The reliable NSU motorcycles that we have in the radio company have provided the best evidence of the quality of your products during our fast advance...."

"... For me it is a particular pleasure that in our messenger platoon we drive nothing but NSU machines...."

On the other hand, the unsuitability of these machines was already being shown in the advancing course of the war during the Russian campaign, as well as in the North African theater of war. In particular, the weather conditions in the vastness of Russia and the sandstorms in North Africa formed insurmountable hindrances for the motorcycles with their limited off-road capability. In addition, the variety of models made the equipping of motorcycles completely impossible. On all fronts there were shortages of necessary spare parts.

This situation improved only as of mid-1941, when the BMW R 75 and Zündapp KS 750 motorcycles, conceived especially for war service, were delivered to the troops by BMW and Zündapp, though only in limited numbers. With their approximately 26 HP, they ranked among the heavy motorcycles. Foot-rest heating for use in the east, additional air filters for use in Africa, plus off-road and reverse gears were just some of the special features of these military motorcycles. As opposed to the street motorcycles originally used, these machines also had appropriate ground clearance. These motorcycles proved themselves thoroughly until the end of the war. Yet it must be said that the BMW and Zündapp designers surely had not reckoned on such weather conditions as the soldiers encountered in the east. This is shown by the first-person story which a BMW designer included in the book "BMW – A German History." The designer recalls this remarkable trip as follows:

"... While we were following the movement of the front in daily stages, we spent the nights in tents on the steppes ... We had crossed the Don and then gone in the direction of Stalingrad, and we sought out the field repair shops, which operated in the most primitive conditions directly behind the front line. There the machines were examined and reports on the troops' experiences were taken. My opinion was correct. The machines went under the liquid mud, which flowed over the motors by the bucketful and was sucked into the low-lying air filter, ruining it – the mud got into the motor, and often the oilpans no longer held oil, but only sand. And the same thing happened to the front-wheel forks, which were not yet protected by rubber shields. It was a fact that on the short trip from our debarking point (Kharkov) to the front, approximately 200 kilometers, the machines were ruined by bad weather and could no longer be used. Nobody brought them back, the repair shop had no spare parts, while there was a gigantic spare-parts depot in Kharkov that did not give out any parts. One saw clearly the enormous difference between the soldiers out there on the front and the back-line people, who were real bureaucrats, while the troops were trying to build one usable machine out of ten ruined ones. –Then we reached Sety, twenty kilometers from Stalingrad – it was still called that then: capturing Stalingrad would have been a snap, but actually this was meaningless; we had reached the Volga! – and from there we moved straight across the Kalmuk Steppe into the Caucasus, or in that direction. We had no problems other than tire defects.... In the Caucasus, the front ran along the Terek. From there we went back via Rostov, to the Sea of Azov, and in Mariopol we were loaded again....

"The new oil filter of my machine, screwed onto the tank high up, performed without trouble. But the improvements – although we worked on them day and night to change the whole series at once –were no longer sufficient for Russia. Stalingrad had changed everything.

"All the machines that went to the east were lost, at least we never heard of them again. We got good reports from Africa. In the desert sand, the new BMW R 75 proved itself very well.... Worse than dust was the liquid mud. I experienced one rainy day – terrible. The clay was so thick that it stuck fast in the hubcaps of the wheels."

The VW Kübelwagen introduced later (as of 1941), or the NSU tracked motorcycle, were no competition as far as maneuverability and driving characteristics in heavy country were concerned. To be sure, the men who drove these vehicles at that time had varying opinions of them.

Equipped with their own crankshaft drive for the sidecar, the two cycles now formed the backbone of the motorcycle rifle units, which had been originated already in 1935. BMW produced a total of 16,500 sidecar machines of the BMW R 75 type, while the total of the KS 750 type built by Zündapp was 18,635. These machines were called "war elephants" in the postwar years. The sidecar machines had made motorcycle history in World War II.

In many armies, most of them European, the trend since the early 1930s had been to make units of the infantry more mobile in the country by using sidecar motorcycles. Cycles made by Gnome & Rhone of France, FN of Belgium, Norton of England, Moto Guzzi and Gilera of Italy and Harley-Davidson of the USA later became the best-known cycles in the European theaters of war. At this time, Germany also began to integrate infantry units mounted on sidecar motorcycles into the army. With the introduction of universal military service, a motorcycle rifle troop was established in the German Wehrmacht in October 1935. It was the intention of the military leadership to move three fully equipped soldiers into position on the foremost front on each sidecar motorcycle as quickly as possible. In the lightning attacks on Poland and France, these motorcycle rifle battalions proved themselves admirably thanks to their intensive off-road training with their cycles. In the tough reality of the war's further events, though, they did not fulfill their combat tasks to the desired extent – the losses of men and material, especially in the Russian campaign, were too high – so that the motorcycle rifle troops were already disbanded before the end of the war. For the most part, the motorcycle riflemen were assigned to the reconnaissance units. On the other hand, the heavy BMW and Zündapp sidecar motorcycles enjoyed the greatest popularity among the actual motorcycle messengers. They were an alternative to the usually light cycles with which they had originally been equipped, and which often got stuck in rough country. Many minor episodes from the everyday events of the war can be recounted by the drivers of these two motorcycles, the BMW R 75 and Zündapp KS 750. For example, in swampy country, the drive wheels were equipped with tire chains, the carburetor setting was adjusted a little higher, and the sidecar motorcycle held a steady speed "through thick and thin" and back to solid ground. The advantage of this trick was that in enemy country, no unnecessary noises were made by the motors, which howled otherwise.

The following documentary photographs shall bear witness to the service of German motorcycles and their drivers in the period from 1935 to 1945. It may be hoped that such scenes will not occur again, and that these will thus remain as unique documents for posterity. Factory and model pictures will contribute to better identification of the motorcycles, often so covered with dirt as to be unrecognizable, in the documentary pictures.

The Training of the Motorcycle Driver

The training of the motorcycle driver took place both in the Wehrmacht and within the framework of pre-military training in the motor sport schools. These were established by the NSDAP, which trained its drivers mainly for the SA. The driving schools were designated NSKK (National-Sozialistische-Kraftfahr-Korps) motor sport schools. Of course a driver did not have to be a member of the NSDAP in order to be trained in driving at these schools. Often there were agreements between the party and the Wehrmacht that regulated motorcycle driver training at one of the NSKK motor sport schools. This pre-military training was particularly vital at that time when there was as yet no military service obligation and volunteer military service lasted only twelve months. This time was nowhere near sufficient to acquire, for example, the required drivers' licenses for all wheeled and tracked vehicles used by an armored reconnaissance unit. Hence the "advance training" in the NSKK motor sport schools.

With the introduction of universal two-year military obligations, more of the driving-school training was carried out in the Army. For this purpose, as a rule, trained driving teachers from the non-commissioned officer corps were available. The training was deliberately very stringent, but for that very reason it later saved many a motorcycle driver's life in combat.

After general driver training on paved roads came off-road training. In part, this was conducted on specially selected areas that challenged all the driver's ability. Wading through waterways, climbing steep slopes or getting through muddy or swampy ground were just some of the difficulties that the student driver had to master. An intensive, drill-like off-road training, involving both solo motorcycles and the heavy sidecar units, was necessary to master the machines thoroughly. The heavy driving-school cycles made by BMW and Zündapp were not easy to handle in roadless areas. Many a student driver who could not keep his machine upright and "went to the ground" had difficulties getting his cycle upright again. In addition, not every driver who had driven a solo machine in civilian life was able to handle the asymmetrical sidecar rig without trouble.

The motorcycle riflemen in particular must be mentioned here. The mistake was and still is made of referring to every motorcyclist who shouldered a carbine as a motorcycle rifleman. This simply is not correct. The motorcycle riflemen were a special type of combat troops who were sent directly into battle with their vehicles, the sidecar motorcycles. As an identifying mark, they bore the tactical symbol of a stylized wheel and handlebars on their sidecar cycles.

In the motorcycle rifle companies, at least 70% of the soldiers were trained as drivers, so that drivers could be changed on long motorized marches. For the training of motorcycle riflemen at the beginning of World War II, there was a lack of good guidelines for training. They came into being only gradually, based on the work of the instructional troops and the collected experiences of the first war years. Thus a motorcycle rifleman's guidebook with illustrations for off-road training of motorcycle crews was in existence, but it never became more than a stopgap measure. Only one instructional and testing unit for the training of motorcycle riflemen was established at Döberitz in 1937. In 1938 it was transferred to Krampenitz and expanded into a cavalry school. The following excerpts will provide a brief overview of the practical training of motorcycle-driving students, including the motorcycle riflemen.

The abbreviation **OSL** referred to certain motorcycles made by NSU in the prewar years and meant: Obengesteuerte Sportmodell Luxus version: overhead-valve sport-model luxury type. The best-known NSU models were the 351 OSL, 501 OSL and 601 OSL. All three types were used in great numbers by the Wehrmacht and will be seen in the illustrations.

Stefan Knittel, the well-known motorcycle journalist, thought up another definition:

Ottos Schöne Liebhaberei *

Again and again, it is the types of motorcycles that were widespread before that turn up only rarely in the hands of old-timer admirers. This is partly because they were simply overlooked years later, because most people remembered the everyday model very well and did not regard it as a rarity. On the other hand, the everyday motorcycles were not preserved and protected after their first few years. When they wore out, they were not stuck away in the garage, but simply thrown out or sold to the junkman.

Otto Cordes of Nordermoor in the Weser Marshes north of Bremen had a lot of contact with agricultural and utilitarian vehicles in his work as a master mechanic. In his spare time, he devoted himself twenty and more years ago to the German motorcycles of the 1930s. He could not just stand and watch while four-stroke sport models that were once in so great demand now simply rusted away. He already had a lot of experience in restoring one after another of them to good-as-new condition. And it also gave him a lot of pleasure. Just looking at the finished machine always pleased him greatly, and he had no objection to taking them on the road either.

In Bremen he was offered a 350 cc NSU around 1979. This 351 OSL cycle made in 1938 (frame number 1 102 311) with its aluminum head was no longer complete, but with a lot of work, Otto Cordes finished the job. A stroke of luck in the same year was the discovery in Hamburg of a second 351 OSL, this one built in 1935 (frame number 886 162). So now he had the two typical models, one with open and one with capsule cylinder head. Since the older one is an early 1935 machine, the valves were still held in their seats by coil springs.

The high-level exhaust system of the earlier NSU was a further fascinating difference. When the time came to photograph it, Otto Cordes remembered that he had wanted for some time to make replacements for the missing perforated rear shields on the mufflers and the bend in the pipe.

He has not driven either of these motorcycles for a long time. But it has remained clearly in his mind that they ran in a straight line very well with their long wheelbase, and that they nevertheless offered playful handling. The relatively high weight was never a disadvantage, for the 350 cc motors were as lively as would be expected from a manufacturer with a good background in racing. When talking about the motorcycles, Otto immediately got the desire to run a few laps. Install batteries, check the air pressure in the tires, fill up with fresh oil, put fuel in the tank and away we go.

* Otto's Beautiful Love Story, from Motorrad Classic, No. 2, 1993.

“The Hat, the Table and the Broom”

A Merry Motorcycle Wager from the Days of World War I

I happened to ask, just few years ago,
A man everyone said would certainly know,
If the motorcycle, in his estimation,
Had a future at all in this war’s operation.
The fellow, who relished an oracle’s role,
First looked at me smiling, a confident soul,
Then after stopping and thinking, he said:
“I’ll give it a year and no more till it’s dead,
But you know, if this period of time has elapsed
And the cycles are not all disposed of and scrapped,
Then I shall eat, without a quibble,
A hat, a table and a broom I’ll nibble.”

I laughed about that, quite naturally,
Asked not a question, but thought privately:
Perhaps the time will come nevertheless,
When I can arrange an occasion, full-dress,
When you, to a skeptical outlook addicted,
Can be reminded of what you predicted.

In the East the cyclist’s lot was not light,
and I often believed the prophet was right,
When I saw a cyclist engulfed in the flood,
Trying to free his machine from the mud.
And when I saw the man around Riga again,
A frustrated cyclist, with puzzled brain,
Stood there with a cycle that just wouldn’t start,
A load on his mind and a pain in his heart.
The man said: “Your faith is delusion, of course,
You can only depend on the great iron horse,
Or a horse with a saddle, if no train’s around,
In no other way can you cover this ground.”

Thus I have seen cyclists, and more than a few,
To whom their clattering bride was untrue,
But everything turned out at last for the best
After the great movement out toward the west.
On smooth roads everything went just fine,
The motorcycle proved to be almost divine,
And I observed, even in pouring rain,
The wheels digging in and moving again.
The hind wheel, of course, skidded left and right,
But in second gear it went, with all its might,
At a steady, unwavering speed with its load
Through the spraying waves of dirt on the road.

I thought very often, and it lightened my gloom,
Of the man eating his hat, table and broom
When I saw motorcycles past me go flitting
Like bolts of lightning on wheels sitting.
And then, on the march through La Fere in the spring,
I met, after three years, the oracle king,
Just as, on the slippery road, muddy brown,
A unit of cycles drove straight through the town.

I pointed to them and I said not a word,
He looked at me blankly, but I knew he heard.
The subject for him was indeed full of pain,

But I could see that he was trying in vain
To find the right words to gain freedom, and fast,
From the duties of being a prophet at last.
I scrounged from a ruined house in the gloom
A hat and a table and even a broom,
And served up the meal at this glorious hour
That he had committed himself to devour
If, after a year had gone by in the war,
Every cycle was not turned to scrap and no more.

Like Shylock, I insisted on getting my due;
About his mistake he was quite full of rue.
And made a remarkably stupid face too –
But eating those objects – that he didn't do!

A war correspondent composed in 1941

The Song of the German Motorcyclist in Africa

Dirty, covered over and over with dust, sweaty, the sleeves of his dust-covered shirt rolled up, there stands a motorcycle messenger before the commander and makes his report. The route that he covered was only ten kilometers. Seventeen times he got stuck in the sand of the desert. By using his last strength, almost in despair, he got his machine going again. He needed almost two hours for these ten kilometers. But he did it, because he had to do it. The lives of many comrades depended on him alone.

Many of the men at the wheels of the cars and trucks, the tanks and the armored scout cars, the cycles and towing tractors went through the campaigns in Poland, Norway, Holland, Belgium or France, but they never faced such difficulties as here in Africa. With its heat, its sandstorms and the sand itself, its rugged country and dust in hitherto unknown quantities, all of that not only has its effect on the material and the motor, but at the same time on the men themselves. Here there is no network of roads, and the marches are therefore 90% desert marches, which cannot be compared with European off-road marches. All of these negative factors have their effect on man and machine. Nature unites them with the enemy.

The physical exertions alone are tremendous. Mercilessly, the sun always joins in, and yet there can be no weariness. Again and again it is said: Push on, either with your own vehicle or with your comrades. The drivers of the solo and sidecar machines have it really rough; their drives in the rolling sandhills are like an antelope's jumps, and in the endless desert sand they consist of alternatingly getting stuck, pushing out and moving forward a few meters.

Perhaps one or another of you will believe this is an exaggeration. Unfortunately, it is not! Ask them some time, the motorcyclists who have sat beside their machines many times, completely in despair, spiritually and physically drained, no longer capable of freeing their cycle from the grip of the sand. Ask them what it is like: Driving a motorcycle in the desert! They do not say much, but their looks speak volumes. It is no disgrace to admit that many of them often gave up hope of escaping from this desert. But comrades' hands have helped again and again, and comrades' words have moved them. Then they moved farther.

Orientation is every bit as hard as driving in the desert. In daylight it is hard enough, at night almost impossible. Without a compass and map it is all but impossible to find your way, for there are scarcely any landmarks by which you can orient yourself. One of the few helpful features are the tracks in the sand, which one must learn to read if one is to trust them.

Tremendous strains are placed on the soldier who has to fight here, and particularly on the German motorcyclist. It must not bother him that he knows that heat, sand, rocks, temperature changes can destroy the tires in a much shorter time than in Europe, that material wears out at an unbelievably fast rate, and that he simply must expect breakdowns at a time when he should otherwise not need to think about them. Here the motorcyclist must be completely one with his task if he is to master it. Of course he was advised with words before he came here, but the reality makes him face unknown demands. Busy as a bee, he must gather experience. The driver must observe, see, hear, and become one with his machine. And therefore there is no rest for him after his service.

The driver is devoted to his vehicle. And when the tremendous power of the Ghibli seizes him on the road, when he must push through sand and dust and wind and heat, kilometer after kilometer, through a hell-born sandstorm, then the man at the controls rises to new heights. Motor and man must suffer, his eyes burn from sand dust, his breath is unsteady, the sweat runs in rivers, and the sand erodes the pulsating motor, the tires reach temperatures up to 70 degrees, and the iron material bends under the constant heat. Thus does the German driver see and experience Africa!

Where would this sentence be more valid than in Africa? How much work, love for one's vehicle, and self-sacrifice go into taking thorough care of a vehicle under such conditions? The drivers have become machines themselves, working machines, and only after their action can them become completely men again! Cursing and complaining, they often stand beside their "manure carts", their "spools", their "mills" and their "dirt sleds", and whatever other pet names there are! And how proud they are of these "beasts" again when they run again, "like a young god."

For the German driver in Africa there are no obstacles, but only gigantic difficulties, but they are mastered!

Honor Their Memory, or in the bad days, Klacks drove a good motorcycle *

At the time of the downfall of the "Thousand-Year Reich", we were allowed to drive motorcycles as messengers in Russia. Or to put it better, we were allowed to devote one third of our days to the sporting discipline of off-road and corduroy-road driving; the second third to the discipline of pushing a motorcycle through the slime, taking the cure by swallowing dust and shoving the cycle, and we spent the last third learning patience while waiting for fuel or spare parts to arrive.

Our mobile seats, BMW R 12, DKW NZ 250/350, NSU 601 OSL, Zündapp KS 600 and whatever else had two wheels, were stripped road machines, unsuited to use in the east. And when, from 1943 on, the secret weapons, the BMW R 75 and Zündapp KS 750, reached us too late and in too small numbers, it was all over.

Among all these street cycles, the DKW NZ 250 and 350 made the best impression – on account of their usefulness. To be sure, the fork springs broke on hard corduroy roads, especially when, from the woods or the skies, the air suddenly, unbearably was filled with iron and lead, and therefore one stepped on the gas and fought with the unbelievably bumping and squirming iron horse. But new fork springs did not grow like heather or steppe grass in that region. Thus one went on driving with the broken one, until such time as one got a new one or found another usable one. Until then, the wild horse did its dance when it hit a tree trunk, rock or the edge of a hole. But the frame didn't break, because the frame bottom of the NZ let it slide over everything. Only the wheel rim could get a dent that had effects, or the air in the tires could disappear for the umpteenth time. The unbelievably reliable

This DKW NZ 350 reflects the catastrophic terrain conditions in the eastern part of the theater of war.

motor always stayed alive. If need be, it even ran on aircraft or captured gasoline and mixtures of 1:20 with stinking used oil from the already grass-grown remains of the offensive of 1941. But the best experience was position five in the ignition lock; there the machine started, even without a battery – in the spring of 1944 I no longer saw an NZ with an intact battery. And today? You can dump a super-modern "bike" at the edge of the road when the twelve-volt reservoir is empty.

* From Motorrad Classic, No. 2, 1993.

The Motor Vehicle Service Medal

In 1942, to recognize the motor vehicle drivers who performed especially noteworthy service in the war – and this automatically included motorcycle drivers – the Kraftfahrbewährungsabzeichen (Motor Vehicle Service Medal) was awarded. The

977th Order on the Establishment of the "Kraftfahrbewährungsabzeichen" of October 23, 1942

was announced in the General Army Announcements of November 21, 1942. The Motor Vehicle Service Medal was awarded in three grades to drivers who had performed special service in the war and under difficult conditions by driving and maintaining the motor vehicles entrusted to them. The medal was worn in the middle of the left lower sleeve and had the following forms:

It was awarded: **in bronze**
in silver
in gold

for service as of December 1, 1940 in the areas of the former Yugoslavia, Greece, Bulgaria, Romania, and in the area eastward of the western boundary of the Soviet Union of 1940 (before the Soviet Union absorbed the Baltic states), in Finland, Norway north of the Arctic Circle or in the area of the German troops serving in Lapland, and in Africa.

It is interesting to note that, in the OKW procedures for awarding the Motor Vehicle Service Medal of October 23, 1942, the motorcycle messengers were named at the head of the list. They could receive the decoration after having proved themselves in ninety days of action under especially rough conditions. When one considers that drivers from Wehrmacht units had to have served 185 days of action before they could be given the medal, it is clear that the particularly demanding service of the motorcycle messengers was being honored here. Thus the account that follows will deal only with the motorcycle drivers.

For days of action to be counted, there had to be difficult conditions of place and action, such as:

- drives under enemy contact,
- particularly great daily accomplishment in terms of distance or vehicle, or particularly difficult road conditions, or
- drives under unusually harsh weather conditions.

The motorcycle drivers had to have excelled by driving sensibly and safely and conscientiously maintaining and servicing their vehicles despite these difficult conditions.

In case of an accident caused by the driver, the previously earned days in action became invalid. Only after six months of trouble-free service could one begin again to count days in action.

An already awarded Motor Vehicle Service Medal was withdrawn in case of

- an accident that was the driver's fault,
- careless vehicle maintenance resulting in damage, or
- exceeding the established speed limit.

Requalifying began exclusively at the lowest, "bronze" level.

The Motor Vehicle Service Medal could be worn on all uniforms and also – in miniature form – on civilian clothing. It was awarded to:

- drivers of the Wehrmacht, as well as
- non-Wehrmacht members subordinated to the Wehrmacht or serving in the occupied areas already named.

The medal could also be awarded to

- foreign volunteers under oath to the Führer and fighting in the Wehrmacht,
- foreign volunteers from the eastern areas liberated from the Communists (including released prisoners of war), as long as they fought for the German Wehrmacht.

Soldiers of allied or friendly nations could not be awarded the Motor Vehicle Service Medal.

During the war the originally named combat areas to which the Motor Vehicle Service Medal was applicable were expanded. On March 9, 1944 the OKW decided that action

- on the island of Sicily as of June 1, 1943,
- on the islands of Sardinia and Corsica as of July 1, 1943,
- on the mainland of Italy south of the Ancona-Piombino line as of August 1, 1943, and
- in Albania as of September 1, 1943

was also included (Army directives, April 8, 1944).

A further extension of the operational area was announced in Army directives of June 21, 1944. As of February 1, 1944, the combat area now included the rearward Army areas and zones of the Army Group North in Estonia, Latvia and Lithuania.

Last but not least, the Army directives of November 21, 1944 stated that the Motor Vehicle Service Medal could be awarded to drivers in service at all fronts in the rearward Army areas and zones designated by Army Group orders as of June 1, 1944, under the specified conditions.

It should be noted that, despite the numerous regulations cited in the Army directives, the possibility of awarding the Motor Vehicle Service Medal to troops at the front were not recognized everywhere. For example, the author known a former Schirrmeister who saw service on all fronts but had no idea that a Motor Vehicle Service Medal even existed. This happened in spite of the fact that in the OKW's instructions for procedure in Ziff. 5 it was specifically stated that drivers' applications for the award were to be examined and submitted by the officers responsible for overseeing the technical maintenance of motor vehicles (such as Schirrmeister).

Paint Schemes

The paint colors of the motorcycles unfortunately cannot be determined with certainty from black and white photographs. Between 1935 and 1945, the colors of paint used on military materials changed several times, so that it is not possible to determine the colors of large-scale military equipment in use during that ten-year period – including motorcycles – today without reference to the Army directives (HM) in force at the time. On the other hand, the many action photographs of motorcycles in "civilian" paint prove that, for various reasons, the prescribed paint colors were not always applied to requisitioned motorcycles. Thus photos of sidecar cycles with black-painted Steib sidecars or NSU cycles with chrome-plated engine-block parts or tank sides are not uncommon. In fact, even motorcycles with chrome-plated exhaust pipes can be found.

By the mid-1930s, a so-called spot camouflage – which clearly separated the individual colors on the vehicle from each other – characterized the appearance of large military equipment. Sidecar machines which are shown in Chapter III – Motorcycle Training – are sometimes painted in this camouflage style, which was taken over from the Reichswehr.

With the establishment of the Wehrmacht in 1935, large military equipment was painted in a considerably darker gray-brown color. At that time, the dark gray color exceeded the dark brown area at a ratio of 2/3 to 1/3. This situation remained in use until the autumn of 1939, so that at the beginning of World War II the German military equipment was painted in this manner. But barely a year after the war began, HM 1940, No. 864 directed that, for reasons of economy, all large equipment should be painted in a single dark gray color for the duration of the war.

It is understandable that, with the expansion of the theater of war in North Africa, this paint color was not suitable for use by the troops operating there.

Thus the OKH directed in its HM 1941, No. 281, that the equipment of the troops serving in Africa should be painted with a camouflage coat of yellow-brown (RAL 800) and gray-green (RAL 7008). Only matte colors were to be used, but they were not to meet each other sharply but gradually mix into each other. The yellow-brown color should predominate. The proportion should be about 2/3 yellow-brown to 1/3 gray-green. Small surfaces (including spoked and disc wheels) could be painted in one color.

The winter camouflage paint used by the troops operating in Norway, Finland and Russia was also specified in an Army directive. Dated November 18, 1941 – and thus much too late – the OKH directed in HM 1941, No. 1128, that all vehicles were to be covered with white paint for camouflage purposes. The paint patterns were left to the troop leaders, but the use of a paint that could be washed off, according to the modified Technical Delivery Specifications 6.345, was called for. The paint had to be sent via the supply routes. But it often reached many troop units too late, so that the troops took it on themselves to paint their vehicles with a chalky fluid that was washed off after the snow had melted. The vehicles then appeared again in the usual dark gray paint. On some motorcycles in the following action photos, this provisional winter paint can be seen clearly. The notorious "Russian Winter of 1942" also caused great problems in terms of camouflage paint. On account of the insufficient supply of suitable camouflage paint, temporary chalk had to be used again and again. Only the units transferred directly from their posts in Germany to the front in the winter had major equipment with prescribed camouflage paint.

In 1942 another change was made in the painting of major equipment. Instead of the previous dark gray paint (HM 1940, No. 864) or the yellow-brown/gray-green paint for use by troops in Africa (HM 1941, No. 281), the equipment – including the motor vehicles of the troops stationed in Africa – was to be painted in brown RAL 8020 and gray RAL 7027 (both colors matte). The proportion was again to be 2/3 brown and 1/3 gray, and here too the colors were to blend into each other. The previously used paint colors, though, RAL 8000 and RAL 7008 (HM 1941, No. 281), were to be used up. These instructions were made known in HM 1942, No. 315.

An essential change from the previous equipment and vehicle paint was introduced at the beginning of 1943. It must be stressed that the major equipment in all theaters of war was given a single-color paint job of dark yellow. In addition, it can be noted in HM 1943, No. 181 and 322, that for the first time the troops were made responsible for painting their large equipment in the suitable camouflage colors for the terrain conditions. For this purpose, three different colors of paste were made available, namely olive green, red-brown and dark yellow. Later a white camouflage paste was added for the wintertime.

The camouflage pastes often had to be thinned with water or gasoline before they could be applied. Thinning with water, though, had the disadvantage that the camouflage paint was washed off very quickly in the rain. On the other hand, if one considers the well-known shortage of gasoline among the troops, no gasoline was available for thinning the camouflage paste. Still this camouflage paste was widely used by the troops.

Color paintings of wartime events made since 1939 and showing German military equipment in a variety of colors thus did not arise from the imagination of the individual artist. They are attributable to the various colors of paint used on the German military equipment over the years. From this it can be concluded that this frequent change in paint colors was not well known, especially to the postwar generations. Thus these depictions not only provide "better recognition" of the following black-and-white photographs, but should also inspire the model builder to present his model motorcycles in the colors that correspond to the appropriate periods of time.

Fall in for inspection! Students at the NSKK Motor Sport School in Tübingen with their BMW R 11 cycles on the parade ground in the spring of 1936. The BMW R 11 was built for the Reichswehr from 1929 to 1934. It had a two-cylinder, 750 cc motor producing 18 horsepower. The training of the drivers and passengers (motorcycle riflemen) was highly valued as pre-military training. During motorcycle training, the crew wore steel helmets with protective strips.

When the war began, the BMW R 4 was the oldest motorcycle in military service. It was used primarily to train driving students, and was already introduced in the Reichswehr in 1932. In numerous off-road competitions at that time, it prepared sport-inspired young men for their duties as motorcycle messengers. Sufficient ground clearance of the motor-gearbox unit and the central stand that folded backward made sure that the cycle did not get upset off the road or even in deep sand. The military version (photo) also had saddlebag attachments and a protective plate at the bottom of the frame.

Intensive motorcycle maintenance was part of all practical off-road training. Here the driving teacher watches his five students during technical service at the Lettow-Vorbeck barracks in Hamburg-Wandsbek in 1938. In the foreground is a BMW R 4, behind it two heavy Zündapp K 800 machines.

Here is a group of cycle and car driving students carrying out technical service. In the foreground is a Wanderer driving school car.

Memories of driving school, 1938: Two BMW R 4 cycles, the five driving school students and their assistant instructor. The cycles displaced 400 cc and produced 12 HP.

Driving teachers of the 7th Company, Infantry Regiment 69 (mot) demonstrate their art with a heavy Zündapp K 800 sidecar model. At public or company events, such acrobatic performances were very popular with the spectators.

A mixed motor vehicle group with their car and BMW R 4 during off-road training. The motorcycle students wear the steel helmet with protective strips. This cycle is an improved version of the R 4, with four-speed transmission shifted by a coulisse on the tank, footrests instead of boards, and a kick starter that could be pushed down in the direction the cycle was to go.

After driving-school training on the road came intensive cycle training in the country. In the foreground are two driving students in long motorcycle messengers' coats, with a Zündapp K 800 sidecar cycle, in the Fischbeker Heide south of Hamburg.

Members of the 3rd Company (motorcycle rifle company) of Reconnaissance Unit 5 (AA 5) during off-road driving training near their base in Eggenburg, Austria in 1939. One matter stressed in off-road training was driving on sandy, rocky and soft ground as well as in bad weather and – as here – in snow. Up to 70% 0f the members of a motorcycle rifle company had been trained on motorcycles.

Bad-weather driving and crossing shallow bodies of water were practiced especially intensively with the sidecar cycles. It must not be forgotten that these were exclusively cycles that were built for use on the road. Driving these machines just as safely off the road demanded much practical experience of the motorcyclists.

Such an "excursion" had to be accepted too. This passenger has obviously left the vehicle unintentionally and "gone swimming." In the spirit of things, he holds his dummy rifle above water, as was practiced countless times in combat training.

Here a motorcycle rifle troop of AA 5 undergoes winter training. In close order, the group is taking a break in its march. Obviously this training was intended only for the further training of the drivers, since there are no passengers.

When you reach the top, let up on the gas! . . .

. . . And when driving down a smooth slope, slow down!

In many theoretical training classes, such procedures were learned by heart in advance. In the country it could then be shown how theory could be turned to practice.

If you can't get up the slope, get out fast, shift down – and push!

Once more, then we'll make it! Such practice was also part of off-road training for motorcycle riflemen.

The driver of this BMW R 12 has placed his body weight on the rear end of the cycle to put more pressure on the drive wheel.

The later fame of the motorcycle riflemen as the "fastest earthbound weapon" was preceded by intensive pre-military driving-school training in trackless areas. If the BMW R 11 rig was able to get through under its own power here, . . .

. . . here the crew had to lend a hand. In the background is the critical driving teacher, who has obviously chosen a particularly swampy terrain for his students.

"Dismount fast!" That was the tactic of the "fastest earthbound weapon", the motorcycle rifleman. They were above all else offensive troops. Reconnaissance, scouting, advance guarding and pursuit of the enemy were their strong points.

Here the motorcycle riflemen are practicing dismounting and taking positions. In field parades and similar events, such demonstrations were willingly given to the public. Later, in war service, speed was essential to survival. In the foreground is the unit's motorcycle messenger on a DKW 350 NZ.

The drivers give the riflemen fire support and take cover behind their machines. As a matter of principle, the drivers did not take part in combat. Their duty was to get the cycles under cover so they could pick up the riflemen again after the battle.

Shallow waters with firm beds were no hindrance for the cycles. Yet it took a lot of skill to take a machine through the water safely without "drowning" the motor.

At that time too, the thorough cleaning of the machine was the last step in daily off-road training. This is a BMW R 11 of 1936.

A motorcycle rifle unit drives through a village. During the war, driving so close together was allowed only in enemy-free areas with full air superiority. The rifleman in the second sidecar wears his rifle strap. The cycles in front are BMW R 12 machines.

Members of the VI. Army Corps on autumn maneuvers in the Lüneburg Heath in 1935. Note the motorcycle crews with their long uniform coats, but with obsolete World War I steel helmets. It is not clear whether or not this is a motorcycle rifle company, as there is no third riflemen on the cycles.

Off-road training for NSKK driving students in the "Ostmark" in 1938. Note the steel helmets with protective strips.

The driving school machines were Zündapp K 500 cycles. The K 500 was used between 1934 and 1938, chiefly by driving schools and later as a communication vehicle in back-line areas.

Military training was also stressed in driving-school training. The cycles – here Zündapp K 500 – and driving students are lined up in marching order (ready to mount!).

Motorized Hitler Youth members with a variety of civilian machines in off-road training. Renowned motorcycle racers of the 1930s were surely models for the young drivers.

The most widespread Wehrmacht cycle was the BMW R 12. It was usually used with a sidecar and displaced 745 cc. This picture shows the modified version with footrests instead of boards.

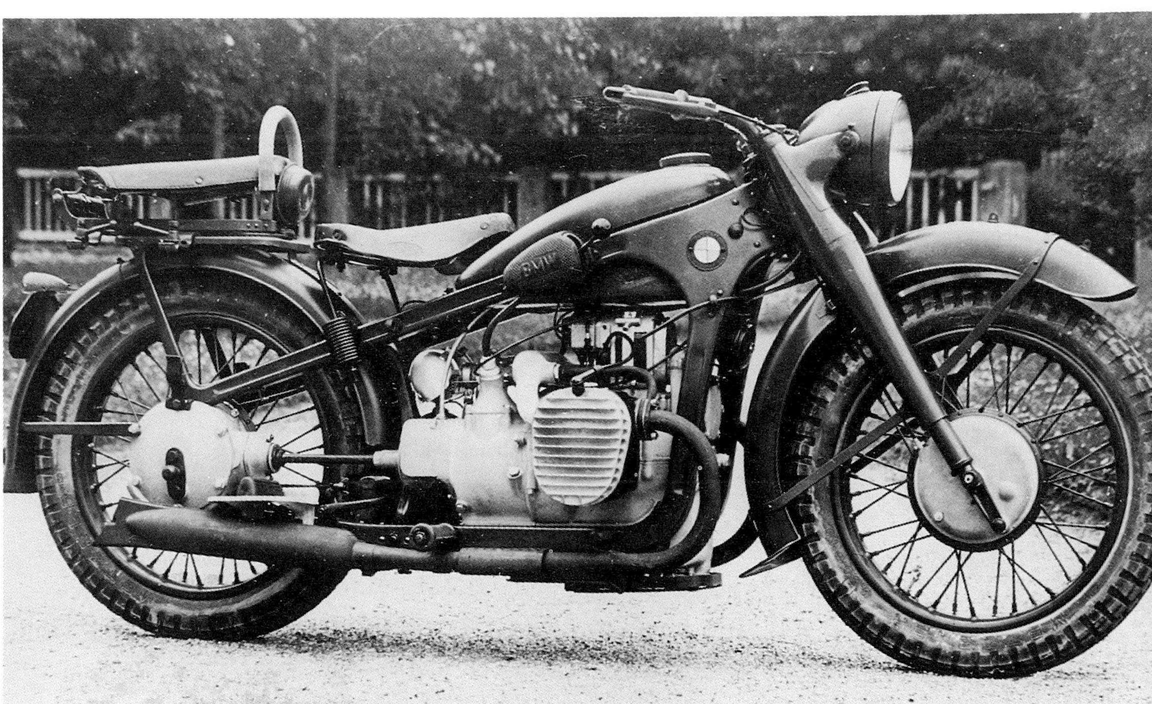

A Zündapp K 800 driving-school cycle of the 7th Company, Infantry Regiment 69 (mot) at the Lettow-Vorbeck Barracks in Hamburg-Wandsbek (1938). The Zündapp K 800 had the largest displacement of any Wehrmacht motorcycle. With its four-cylinder opposed motor (22 HP), the solo cycle weighed 215 kilograms. This machine was very popular among the troops.

Parade formation of parts of a motorcycle rifle company with their BMW R 11 cycles, circa 1934. At that time the sidecars still had opening side doors. The crew was equipped with World War I steel helmets.

The unit's Schirrmeister has obviously hurried to appraise the damage to the tracked vehicle that has turned over. The cycle is a Zündapp KS 600 W of the 2nd Repair Shop Company of a supply battalion. In the background are two Ju 52 planes.

The crew of this BMW R 12 drives casually along a mountain road in Norway. On the basis of the WM 2588 number, the cycle and its crew are under the command of the Baltic Sea Naval Station at Kiel.

A good view of the "shining clean" BMW R 75 in the German Museum in Munich. Special features of this 1942-43 machine include the rubber bellows on the front fork, rough-tread tires, and high air filter for use in Africa.

A motorcycle messenger with typical equipment, on his DKW 350 NZ. The pouch is part of his personal equipment, as is the long messenger's coat.

The motorcyclists pushed their way through roadless woods and fields on cycles not built for off-road use, under constant danger of flank attacks. Often everyone had to help move one machine after another through impassable terrain (Russia, 1941).

Motorcycle messengers meet members of a spare-parts store unit in Königsberg in 1940. The picture shows two NSU cycles with civilian Steib sidecars, requisitioned from private owners.

While the engineers are still building the bridge, the motorcycle riflemen are already crossing it. Speed was typical of these fighting troops.

This light messenger's cycle, a German Triumph (TWN) B 200, was very rarely seen. The machine was built in 1936 and 1937 and displaced only 196 cc. This is obviously a requisitioned cycle.

Times change! In the background are traditional horsedrawn wagons, in front the motorcycle messenger with his Zündapp K 500. This is obviously a requisitioned cycle, as civilian dirt catchers and a civilian Steib sidecar were not found on military vehicles. The headlight cover is also only temporary. This picture was taken in 1940.

This BMW sidecar carries an MG 34 on a folding mount. The standard machine gun used by the motorcycle riflemen was the MG 34 (7.92 caliber). It was attached to a mount on the sidecar and thus could be used to hold back the enemy while the cycle was moving.

The drivers and passengers regularly used breaks in marches to get some much-needed rest. The cycles are BMW R 12 machines.

A motorcycle messenger on his Zündapp K 500. Most of the motorcycles delivered to the Army by Zündapp from 1934 to 1939 were K 500 machines. The cycle looks very rugged, but it had only a 250 cc motor. The civilian IP registration indicates that this was a requisitioned machine from Prussia (Schleswig-Holstein Province).

Often the drivers had time for just a short nap on their cycles. At left is probably a Puch S 4, at right a BMW R 12. The drivers wear long messengers' coats.

When the rainy season set in, almost all roads turned to seas of mud. Officers and men are working together here to get the cycle going again.

"Messengers have to get through everywhere!" A propaganda postcard from the Wehrmacht High Command.

Motorcycle riflemen of the 5th Panzer Division in the Balkan campaign of 1941. Although the cycles bear the tactical symbol of the motorcycle riflemen, the crews are not complete.

A reconnaissance unit, mostly with BMW R 12 cycles, at rest.

Help is needed to get the heavy Zündapp KS 600 W going again. One can see the toughness in the motorcycle messenger's face. In the first campaigns against Poland and France, the motorcyclists found a relatively intact network of roads, so that their cycles, which were exclusively civilian machines, were not exposed to any particularly bad conditions. That was to change radically in Russia.

With all their strength they push the cycle onto the damaged wooden bridge . .

. . . and off the other end. Note the tactical symbol of the motorcycle riflemen on the sidecar, the stylized wheel with stylized diagonal handlebars.

This crew has camouflaged their BMW R 75 cycle to fit into the snowy landscape better. Note the modified version of the cycle, with rubber bellows on the front fork. Chalk was obviously used in place of paint. Note also the crew's snow suits.

A motor park scene. At right is an NSU 601 OSL with the big tank filler cap for canister filling, at left a BMW R 61, which was made for the Wehrmacht from 1938 to 1941.

Here again, combined efforts are needed to get this BMW R 75 with sidecar out of the mud. The rubber bellows on the front fork show that this is a 1942-43 cycle.

A strong scouting troop of the 5th SS Panzer Division waits for orders. The rough tread of the front tire on the first motorcycle is easy to see.

This motorcycle messenger, seen on his NSU 351 OSI, was an employee of the NSU cycle paint shop as a civilian and sent this photo to his former fellow workers.

This motorcycle and sidecar were obviously no obstacle to a tracked vehicle.

Messengers and scouts of a battalion of the "Grossdeutschland: Panzer Grenadier Regiment (Russia, 1942). The solo cycles are DKW 350 NZ. A barefoot boy with a big cap stands beside the road and stares wide-eyed.

Motorcycle messengers in their typical long raincoats on BMW R 12 machines in Greece, 1941.

Members of a reconnaissance unit with their NSU 601 OSL cycles pass through a town deserted by the civilian population.

Men of Motorcycle Rifle Battalion 19 with their BMW R 12 cycles in Russia in 1942. The MG 34 mounted on the sidecar and its 50-round belt drum are easy to see. Men and machines have obviously been through rough times.

A makeshift repair shop for motorcycles. In front are the remains of a Zündapp cycle with Steib civilian sidecar, behind it an NSU 351 OSL. Repairing motorcycles in the field often took place – as can be seen clearly here – under very primitive conditions. On account of the variety of models, there was a great shortage of spare parts.

Enemy in sight! After the riflemen dismount, the drivers quickly take cover with their sidecar cycles (Russia, 1942).

A Zündapp K 800 sidecar cycle of Engineer Battalion (mot) 38 of the 2nd Panzer Division in the French campaign in 1940. Concentrating intensely, the man in the sidecar holds his carbine ready to fire. Yet the driver does not dispense with his cigar.

In remembrance! A motorcycle messenger and his comrades on a civilian NSU 501 OSL. Note that the sides of the tank and the exhaust pipes are chromed. The unstraightened fishtail end of the exhaust pipe also indicates a civilian machine. The civilian registration (III D- for the districts of Leonberg and Ludwigsburg, the police chief of Heilbronn) also shows that this is a requisitioned machine.

The driver and his BMW R 12 cycle are sunk equally deep in the mud. This picture shows that heavy motorcycles had their problems in swampy ground.

This picture shows that the German soldiers were often welcomed as liberators in the Baltic republics and western Ukraine. Here the crew of a Zündapp, probably a K 800, is greeted. Note that a spare canister of fuel is carried on the sidecar instead of packs. The crew belonged to the 16th Panzer Division in the Army Group von Kleist (K).

This motorcyclist, seen on his BMW R 16 with Steib civilian sidecar, has replaced his heavy steel helmet with a light hat.

Army doctors also appreciated the mobility of a sidecar cycle. This NSU 601 OSL with red cross emblem on the sidecar is being used by a doctor, who has set up his dressing station in a central location near the battalion's command post.

Motorcycle riflemen respond to an air-raid alarm. In the middle is an NSU 501 OSL, very popular before the war as a powerful sporting machine.

Motorcycle riflemen of a reconnaissance unit with their BMW R 12 cycle beside a column of prisoners. The cycle is the unmodified version, with wide protective plate and aluminum footboards. The machine-gun belt is very easy to see.

Supply bombs are transported on a BMW R 75 machine.

This mountain is too steep for the cycles. The motorcycle riflemen's machines are towed uphill by a self-propelled 2 cm Flak gun.

Motorcycle messengers in the fog (France, 1941). These men, whether messengers, traffic guides or scouts, performed a great service for the military command in all units, in all theaters of war.

The obviously solid bottom allows this driver to ford a pond safely with his NSU 601 OSL.

For the family album. Two cycle crews, photographed in France in 1940.

The big "G" on the sidecar identifies these resting cycle crews as members of the Guderian Panzer Group (France, 1941).

Obviously, contact with the enemy has not been made yet, as the motorcyclists have parked their cycles out in the open and the drivers are moving around freely in the country.

These motorcycle riflemen do not have to go into action yet, as the wrapped-up machine gun on the cycle at right indicates.

Obviously in a good mood, these cycle crews enjoy a meal and share their newest war experiences. The driver of the BMW R 12 has stored two stick grenades behind the headlight of his cycle (France, 1940).

The heavy BMW R 75 machines are carrying riflemen. The wide tires are especially noteworthy. They were like those of the VW Kübelwagen.

Motorcycle riflemen advancing through a destroyed village.

Field policemen on a BMW R 12 in Russia in 1941.

Field police show a motorcycle messenger the way (France, 1940). Above an NSU 601 OSL, below the solo 501 OSL.

Despite good ground clearance and wide tires, the sidecar cycles had problems in soft ground (Russia, autumn 1943). In the swamps created by autumn rain and after the snow melted in the Russian theater of war, the motorcycle riflemen, once known for their speed, confronted unimaginable terrain conditions.

Solo and sidecar cycles accompany the advance of armored vehicles (Russia, 1941). Motorcycle messengers were an important element in the conduct of combat.

A motorcycle rifle unit in a surprise attack on a Russian village in 1941.

Motorcycle riflemen of the 12th Panzer Division advancing in Russia in 1941. This rifle platoon is led by the platoon leader's car, followed by three rifle groups with sidecar cycles. For anti-aircraft defense, a machine gun was mounted on a tripod in the platoon leader's car, so fire could be opened on low-flying attackers immediately.

A reconnaissance unit moves into a Russian village to rest (June-July 1941). The picture shows hectic activity in the rest area.

Motorcycle riflemen on their BMW R 12 cycles cross a desert area in North Africa (April 1941). The R 12 was not yet equipped with a high air filter – like the later R 75 – thus dust and sandstorms did much damage to the motor.

With great care, this cycle crew approaches a deserted farm with rifles ready to fire.

The heavy Zündapp KS 750 with its grim-looking passenger.

A Russian farm goes up in flames after a battle (summer 1941). The motorcycle riflemen were specially trained for surprise attacks.

This crew of paratroopers – recognizable by their helmets – gets a little rest on their BMW R 12 cycle in Russia in 1942.

The messenger on his NSU 351 OSL brings an important message. The messenger was naturally a "lone fighter." A good sense of direction and capability in handling their cycles typified these soldiers.

This NSU 351 OSL already has a tapered fishtail exhaust pipe, so that the uniform saddlebags, which are missing here, could be attached without problems.

The food bringer, Obergefreiter Spohner of Heavy Artillery Regiment 84, on an NSU 351 OSL, returns to his unit on the Channel coast in 1941. When the field kitchens of the combat units could not follow them, or when parts of a unit were serving in advanced positions, their food – the familiar casserole, as a rule – was put into thermos containers and delivered by any available vehicles. Here the motorcycle messenger, always ready for action, came through again.

Even when the fender of the sidecar is missing, the cycle fender and sidecar are dented and the headlight cover is lost, this sidecar cycle is not about to be dumped into the ocean!

Motorcycle messengers – whether as couriers, traffic guides or scouts – made an undeniable contribution to the conduct of the war in all types of units in all theaters of war. When other means of communication failed, they came through!

Motorcycle riflemen carry a light machine gun on an "adjustable mount" on their sidecar. This allowed them to fire "from the vehicle", even while in motion if necessary. This is a BMW R 11 with MG 13, circa 1935.

A folding wooden chair serves as a makeshift writing desk. In the background is a civilian BMW R 5, a requisitioned cycle in gloss black paint.

Motorcycle messengers of a reconnaissance unit pause in the market place of a French city in 1940.

A field postcard of the "Unsere Wehrmacht" series, showing a motorcycle rifle crew on a BMW R 11 with sidecar in 1934. Note the sidecar's side door with handle and the mounted MG 13. The two-tone paint of the old Reichswehr can also be seen.

Members of the von Kleist (K) Army Group with a Zündapp K 800 in France in 1940. One can see that they have been through rough conditions.

At times motorcycles were also used as command vehicles by the leaders of unit parts. Here the Schirrmeister of the 7th Company, Infantry Regiment 69 (mot) and his motor vehicle locksmith are seen on their Zündapp K 800 while going to help a damaged vehicle. Obviously "one heart and one soul."

Field Marshal von Kluge, Commander of the 4th Army, on an inspection trip at the eastern front in 1941. His messengers – seen here on BMW R 35 cycles – wear an overlay with crossed marshal's batons on the chest and back.

Cycles in Africa! In this theater of war too, great demands were made on men and materials. Congested air filters put many motorcycles out of action (Tunisia, 1942).

September 1939: The war is just a few days old. German troops are advancing in Poland. In the foreground is a BMW R 12 messenger's cycle with the standard of the troop leader.

The horse-drawn supply troops follow the advancing combat units (Poland, Sept. 1939). At right is a motorcycle messenger on his NSU 501 OSL.

This interesting picture shows Romanian motorcycle messengers on German Zündapp cycles during the German-Romanian offensive in Bessarabia (July 1941, advance on Kishniev).

The motorcycle rifleman's "runway", a railroad track. The drivers needed much ability to avoid damage to their cycles. Here the driver's intensive training paid off. In the foreground is a BMW R 12 with an MG 34 mounted on the sidecar.

A requisitioned DKW NZ 350. The chromed tank, lack of chain covers, shortened exhaust pipe, small headlight and missing rear portion of the fender indicate a civilian machine (Matrenino, Russia, November 1941).

This motorcyclist with his civilian Steib sidecar passes a mounted unit in the Somme area of France, June 7, 1940.

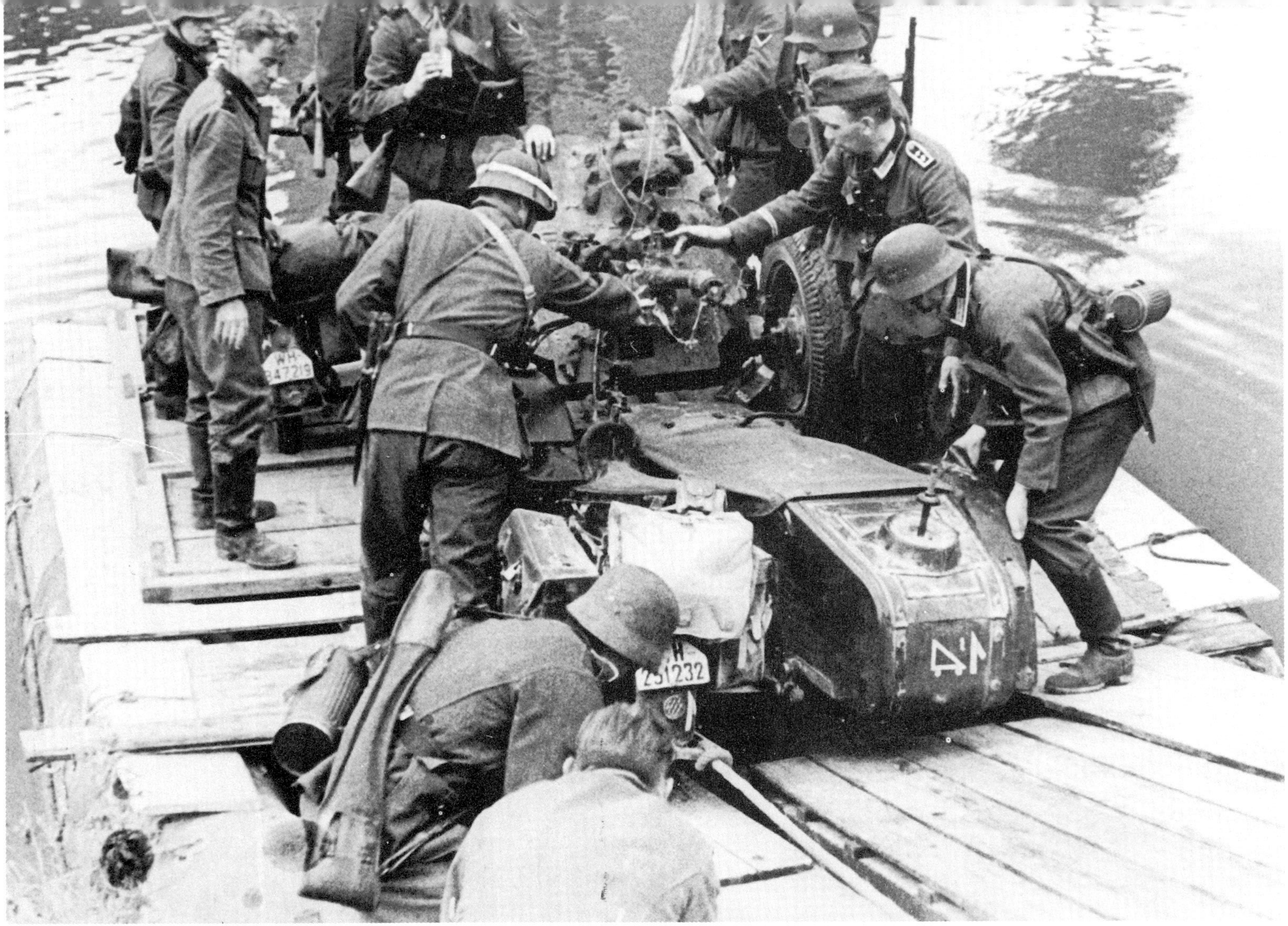

Sidecar cycles are loaded onto a rubber boat to be ferried across the Aisne. One of the cycles is obviously used to tow an infantry gun (France, June 1940).

Wholly or partly destroyed bridges were often given makeshift repairs so that light vehicles such as motorcycles and bicycles could cross them. Here a sunken barge has been turned into a makeshift bridge across the Maas-Schelde Canal. In the foreground is a BMW R 12, at left a DKW NZ 350 (France, May 25, 1940).

When no bridge was available, the motorcycle crews set up their own rubber-boat ferries to get their vehicles across (France, June 1940).

This picture shows what burdens the motorcycles were exposed to. Naturally, most of the cycles – which were civilian road models –were not equal to this pressure. Here a mountain Jäger unit marches into the Sudetenland (October 2, 1938).

This interesting photo shows requisitioned cycles in their original paint. At left is a BMW R 61. This machine was not among those made for Wehrmacht use. Third from right: a BMW R 12 with a huge fender. The Wehrmacht version had a smaller fender in place of it (Poland, 1939).

The heavy Zündapp KS 750 with a Russian crew in Berlin in 1945. The machine has a Russian license plate, but still has well-preserved knobby off-road tires.

Returning from a scouting mission, these motorcyclists fall back into their unit's marching formation (Rzeka-Bug, Russia, June 22, 1942).

A courier with his driving-school helmet on a BMW R 4 cycle.

This picture expresses the coldness of the Russian winter. The BMW R 51 has already suffered from the weather conditions. The front fender and headlight cover are missing.

A Polish retreat route between Przysucha and Radom on September 8, 1939. In the foreground is a BMW R 35 medium Wehrmacht cycle. This 350 cc BMW with undamped telescopic fork was made in great numbers for the Wehrmacht beginning in 1937.

The motorcyclists use the tall sunflowers as cover when the enemy approaches. An ammunition case can be seen on the sidecar of the BMW R 75 (sunflower field near the Caspian Sea, October 1942).

Not a flower market, but a friendly greeting for a unit returning from the front in France. At left is a DKW NZ 350, at right an NSU 251 OSL (Munich, July 16, 1940).

On July 3, 1940 the people of Krefeld welcome the returning 6th Panzer Division at its garrison after the French campaign.

Despite its red cross markings, this medical column was attacked and wiped out. Only the NSU 501 OSL cycle and its Steib sidecar have remained unharmed. The cycle was also marked with a red cross (Western Front, 1944).

When the machine gunner wants to fire, he calls to the driver, "I'm going to shoot!" A picture taken during maneuvers.

The staff of an anti-aircraft unit repairs its motorcycles in Russia in 1941.

This member of the repair troop of the 1st company of a 3.7 cm anti-aircraft battery quietly repairs a DKW NZ 350 (Greece, spring 1941). The field repair troops often had major problems because they lacked spare parts.

Together we are strong. That was especially true of motorcycle riflemen who very often were able to move their cycles through trackless terrain only with the help of all. Notice the added protective bar attached ahead of the cylinder (Russia, early July 1941). In the east, motorcycle riflemen had not only the enemy opposing them. Under the difficult geographical conditions of eastern Europe, they very quickly lost their real stock in trade, speed. Their heavy sidecar cycles were not designed for such terrain conditions.

At the obelisk on the Place de la Concorde in Paris, the populace observes the German soldiers marching in. At right is a Zündapp, at left an NSU 601 OSL (June 14, 1940).

Beer tastes good out of any vessel. This group has tapped their keg at the back of a Russian cabin and drinks it out of cooking-pot lids. In the center is a BMW R 12 (Russia, 1942).

Here again is the BMW R 12 with the big fender which was given up because it got clogged with dirt too fast. The footboards were later replaced by footrests too.

Comradeship radiates from this photo. The motorcycle crews in particular were an inseparable team on their machines. Here they sit on their NSU 601 OSL and exchange the day's experiences.

Is the wading ability of the BMW R 12 being tested in mud here? Surely not. Such terrain was an everyday occurrence in Russia (October 18, 1942).

The repair troops repaired motorcycles in the field. In the foreground is a DKW NZ 350 on blocks, with obvious damage to the front wheel. The lowest level of motorcycle service during the war was regular service and maintenance. The motorcyclists either were well prepared in their driving-school training, or they knew their cycle thoroughly because it had been their own before it was requisitioned.

Motorcycle messenger Leonhard Spohrer of Heavy Artillery Regiment 84 on his NSU 351 OSL. It is a requisitioned machine with civilian registration IH (for the province of Pomerania) and the official WH (Wehrmacht-Heer) marking.

Motorcycle Messenger Spohrer in his long rubberized messenger's coat, with his message pouch and holster for the P 38 pistol. The NSU 351 OSL has a high exhaust pipe. The tank obviously has side extensions, which were available in this form on civilian machines since 1936.

Motorcycle messengers of Heavy Artillery Regiment 84 after the winter combat near Leningrad in 1942. The picture was taken at Zeitz in 1942 on the occasion of the regiment's return to repair equipment. At left is an NSU 351 OSL, at right a DKW NZ 350. The motorcycle messengers' long coats were either worn open or . . .

. . . worn around the legs similar to trousers, as in this picture, so that they offered good protection against wind and weather.

Its owner's pride: his requisitioned BMW R 51, highly polished. According to its numbering, its driver was stationed in Military Zone VI, Münster, Westphalia.

A motorized unit crosses the Loire near Orleans in june 1940. In the center is an NSU 601 OSL with civilian sidecar, behind it a BMW R 12. This railroad bridge was built for use by agricultural vehicles as well.

Armed with his MP 40, this motorcycle messenger poses for the photographer on his battle-scarred Zündapp K 600 W. The MP 40 was one of Germany's best-known infantry weapons. Only sustained fire was possible with it.

The questions of a battalion commander often consisted of: "Where are enemy antitank guns? Where are mines? Can we get through?"

The motorcycle messenger's long coat of rubberized fabric was particularly practical for the motorcyclists on their unprotected cycles. Notice too the complete cover of the headlight of this BMW R 12.

A look at the motorcycle collection of K. H. Denzler in 8546 Thalmässing. Mr. Denzler has one of the largest collections of motorcycles from the pre-1945 era.

When radio silence was ordered, either light signals or motorcycle messengers were used to transmit orders. Often the messengers had to hurry from one command post to another, without any fire cover, to deliver important messages. If all other means of communication failed, then it was all up to the motorcycle messenger.

Most motorcycle messengers knew their machines inside and out, as can be seen here. As long as no major spare parts were needed, they made their own repairs, as here to a requisitioned Puch S 4 with an Austrian Felber sidecar. The canoe-like nose and the bar over the front were typical of this brand of sidecar.

Many repairs had to be made to hard-pressed motorcycles beside the road and as quickly as possible. This particularly applied to the motorcycle messengers and their machines in case of a flat tire, as with this Zündapp K 500. The folding fender allowed easy removal of the wheel.

In a rest area, the motorcycle riflemen quickly camouflaged their cycles with tent canvas, branches, straw and the like to blend into the surroundings. These soldiers have also set up their two-man tent. Notice the small mascot at the peak of the tent.

The motorcycle messenger and his tasks:

– Scouting routes, roads, technical stops, rest areas, gathering places
– Transport of unit commanders and ordnanze officers
– Accompanying and directing marching columns
– Communication with neighboring troops

Many a civilian owner's hard-earned sidecar cycle met a cruel fate when requisitioned for Wehrmacht use. In rough front action it was sometimes no longer recognizable, as will probably happen to this NSU 601 TS with its Steib sidecar. The sidecar was listed in the prewar Steib catalog as Sport Sidecar No. 31 and featured bumper bars all around.

When the motorcyclists could expect low-flying enemy aircraft, they wore a Schiffchen or peaked cap on the road. The broad rim of the steel helmet prevented them from hearing the sounds of aircraft engines in advance. In the foreground is a BMW R 75 of 1942-43.

Motorcycle messengers of the Guderian (G) Panzer Group have taken cover beside a house with their various motorcycles.

Low-flying planes can be expected. These two paratroopers in their "bone bags" – as their camouflaged fatigues were called – stop their Zündapp K 800 to read the information on a road sign.

When a combat or supply unit stopped to rest, covered areas alongside the marching route were occupied. Entry into a rest area was controlled by motorcycle messengers.

This motorcycle messenger sits by his Zündapp cycle in an obviously enemy-free area and perhaps dreams of his family back home.

Motorcycle messengers moved back and forth between troop units during troop transfers. In the process, they often covered several hundred kilometers per day. This messenger is driving a Zündapp K 600.

A postcard from the "Our Army" series, circa 1935. The motorcyclist on his BMW R 11 still wears a helmet with padding; his passenger and the other men wear World War I steel helmets.

Wehrmacht members who went into service with their requisitioned NSU sidecar cycle and here are surely filling up for the last time at a civilian gas station. The IA registration stands for the State Police District of Berlin.

Warm feet below – hot soup above! With his feet on the warm engine block, this motorcycle messenger eats his hot casserole from the cooking pot. The "first-generation" BMW R 12 still has footboards instead of footrests.

The mud seasons of spring and fall were particularly overwhelming in the east. The mud crippled all movements, both in marching and combat. This motorcycle messenger and his NSU 601 OSL try to fight their way through the bad weather conditions.

Here the cycle crew has obviously given up trying to repair their Zündapp for the time being and paused for a meal. The terrain in which the motorcyclists had to operate is unimaginable. In their first campaigns in Poland and France, the motorcycle riflemen found a relatively good and intact network of roads, so that their cycles, which were exclusively civilian machines, were not exposed to any very great demands. That was to change radically in Russia.

The one-cylinder BMW R 4, with pressed steel frame and leaf springs, displaced 400 cc. Since 1932 it ranked among the machines with the best roadholding and, not without reason, was chosen overwhelmingly for driving-school use.

This proud messenger's Zündapp cycle, seen on the market place of a French city, is already equipped with knobby tires.

This BMW R 12 does not appear to have encountered any front duty. Its body and paint are still in perfect condition.

Toughness can be seen in this driver's face. Did he simply put on his uniform jacket and steel helmet to pose for a photo on his civilian DKW NZ 350? His shoes, the unusual headlight cover, and the civilian IA registration (State Police District Berlin) leave us in doubt.

This Luftwaffe motorcycle messenger and his BMW R 35 have obviously been through rough times in trackless country. The 35o cc BMW replaced the BMW R 4 as a medium Wehrmacht cycle in 1937. More than 15,000 of this model were built between 1937 and 1940, but very few of them were sold to private individuals.

Members of a reconnaissance unit of the 6th Panzer Division advance southward across the Aisne near Rethel on June 10-11, 1940. The fight for the town is over. The reconnaissance unit gathers to be given new assignments.

Motorcycle riflemen precede the column of the Reich Protector of Bohemia and Moravia on the Charles Bridge in Prague – coming from Hradschin – where the ceremony of the Protector's installation had taken place on April 16, 1939.

Lunch break for a mobile unit on the Berlin Ring in 1939. In the foreground is a BMW R 61 with a Steib sidecar and the civilian IA registration (State Police District Berlin).

Motorcycle messengers with their DKW NZ 350 at their base. the NZ was a reliable cycle for messengers. The Wehrmacht requisitioned a great many of this type and used them for courier duty.

The nimble cycles were used for quick courier missions. Here the motorcycle messenger, on his Zündapp KS 600, picks up a hastily obtained spare part that was flown in by air courier service.

This motorcycle messenger drives a captured British Ariel cycle. The chromed exhaust pipe and light front wheel suggest a formerly civilian machine.

A blown tire on a DKW NZ 350. The fender is hinged to allow removal of the rear wheel, and is held in place by a lever.

The assembled motorcycle messengers with their various solo and sidecar machines are waiting here for further orders. Unit leaders have obviously called them in for a situation conference. For such trips, the fast and handy motorcycles were usually used.

A captured Belgian cycle, the Gillet 750. This 1938-40 machine had its own side-car drive. The Gillet was the most frequently used cycle in the Belgian Army.

Another picture of the captured Belgian Gillet 750 machine. This cycle had a foot-shifted five-speed gear-box (four forward speeds plus reverse).

The motorcycle messenger of a supply unit, on a cycle that cannot be identified precisely, is seen on a road in Norway (winter 1942). Note the wrappings on the handlebar grips, plus the two saddlebags on the front fork and the loaded fender.

Unimpressed by the destroyed vehicles beside the road, a motorcycle messenger steers his BMW R 12 along the supply route.

The Zündapp KS 600 W cycle was built until mid-1941 and was more popular among drivers than the BMW R 12. According to its registration, it belonged to Air District Command XIII in Nürnberg.

These vehicles were obviously prepared for a propaganda exhibition. The picture includes a 1938 BMW R 51 with a civilian license plate, with the B for Braunschweig (from Kennzeichen für Reichsgaue bzw. kleine Länder).

Members of the LAH unit at their motorcycle repair shop. In the foreground is the driveshaft of a BMW machine. The repair troop of every unit often had its hands full of work in trying to make the cycles ready for action again despite the shortage of spare parts.

Members of the Guderian (G) Panzer Group studying maps. The sidecar cycles were especially useful for reconnaissance and scouting in the country. With their off-road capability and small silhouette, they were far better suited to these tasks than the slower and noisier SPW. A Zündapp cycle is at left.

This is another captured Belgian motorcycle. The Belgian firm of Sarolea put its Type 1000 on the market in 1939.

The Sarolea was the first cycle that had a differential. When it was engaged, one could drive in circles with the cycle.

A captured FN motorcycle from Belgium. The renowned Belgian firm of Fabrique National introduced this model to the army in 1938. In addition to its three-man crew, the machine could carry a load of 300 kilograms.

A rare sight! At left a BMW R 61 with sidecar, driven by a motorcycle messenger with a unique form of face protection that was not customary in the Wehrmacht. The front fender of the R 61 is already missing. Behind it is a Zündapp K 600.

Unser Heer
Schnelle Truppen: Kradschützen auf dem Vormarsch

Feldpost No 58391 - B.

Another postcard from the "Unser Heer" series: "Fast troops: Motorcycle riflemen on the advance." The sender added his field post number to the card.

Motorcycle messengers on NSU cycles in the streets of Bruges after the surrender. In front is an NSU 351 OSL, behind it an NSU 601 OSL.

In 1943 the Reichspost still portrayed the impressive fighting spirit of the German motorcycle riflemen thus. Aside from the fact that the motorcycle riflemen no longer existed at that time, the picture shows an obsolete cycle, a BMW R 11 from the mid-1930s.

These two soldiers pose proudly on their requisitioned Horex S 5 in front of their family's home. The cycle still bears its HH civilian registration (for Hamburg), and was advertised in prewar days as "the motorcycle for the sportsman."

These men in a back-line area of the front are able to relax. The driver has put his feet up, his shirtless passenger is reading, and the third member of the team is airing out his 'Knobelbecher' boots. In the center is the BMW R 35 medium messenger cycle.

Several male inhabitants of this town obviously had to clean the market place for an assembly of German troops. In the foreground is the BMW R 35 medium messenger cycle.

Only a short nap! The enemy must not be given a chance to form its defenses. Here the NSU 601 OSL cycles serve as places to rest.

The shortage of roads on the wide plains of Russia often demanded much from the motorcyclists on their machines, which were not built for off-road use, such as this BMW R 12.

Mud, dust and catastrophic road conditions did not make advancing any easier for the cycles.

In the extremely low temperatures of the Russian winter, the motorcyclists on their unprotected vehicles suffered particularly. Here we see the crew of a BMW R 12. Note the night-marching device on the sidecar and the driver's helmet.

German troops pushed forward ceaselessly in the south Russian steppes. At right is a Puch S 4 messenger's cycle. The machine displaced 250 cc and was ranked as a light motorcycle.

A blond soldier on his heavy Zündapp KS 750. Note the knobby tires and the missing headlight lens.

This motorcycle messenger on his Zündapp K 800 cycle proudly shows his military medal. A messenger was often the last link in the chain of command to the foremost positions, and his bravery was shown in many situations.

These soldiers look a bit bewildered after having removed the rear wheel of their Zündapp KS 750 cycle.

Although this photograph was certainly not taken by a professional, one can still see the big front fender with which the BMW R 12 was supplied to the Army as of 1935.

A British Norton 16 CS, probably captured at Dunkirk, given a Wehrmacht registration and utilized as a light messenger cycle.

This crew is obviously happy with their captured Belgian Rene Gillet cycle. This machine was used primarily as a military and police vehicle in its homeland. Note the temporary identifying mark and the damaged headlight.

This cycle crew and their captured French Terrot 500 ohv cycle have finished a long march through dusty country. They have protected their respiratory organs from sand and dust with cloths over their mouths and noses. Their faces show the conditions under which the soldiers had to travel on their unprotected cycles. During the week-long marches and battles, the motorcyclists, who had to pass the vehicle columns numerous times because of their missions to deliver messages, had to swallow a lot of dust on the Russian roads and steppes.

Is this a French Terrot 500 OHV motorcycle? Can anyone identify it for sure?

The motorcycle messenger and his friend pose for a photo in front of the ruins of a Polish produce company's building.

This civilian cycle and its Steib sidecar were badly damaged when the wooden bridge caved in (Poland, 1940).

The abandoned BMW R 35 cycle of a German motorcycle messenger is passed by a column of prisoners.

This crew, dressed in their fatigue uniforms, also rides a requisitioned Puch (Poland, 1940).

A motorcycle rifle battalion turns out at Bad Kissingen in 1937. This picture shoes the great numbers of cycles in a motorcycle rifle battalion at that time.

A cycle and sidecar not found among Wehrmacht vehicles. This police crew has mounted a hand-driven siren on their sidecar, so they can still give an air-raid alarm in case their regular siren breaks down.

A motorcycle rifle unit passes a Russian village. In the foreground is a BMW R 12 with an MG 34 mounted on the sidecar. Pursuit of the enemy was one task of the motorcycle riflemen where they could utilize the speed and mobility of their sidecar cycles.

The leg protectors over the cylinders of this BMW R 75 cycle are easy to see, but the headlight cover is missing.

The American Harley-Davidson WLA 45 wartime model in 1:9 scale. Note the dirt catcher extending to the height of the driver's chest, plus the holster and gun on the side.

The detailed motor area of the sand-tan Harley-Davidson WLA 45. The footboards instead of foot-rests were typical of the Harley. This model kit is particularly well suited to fans of filigree work.

The light British Triumph messenger's cycle, painted sand tan, with a symbol of an elephant on the saddle bag to indicate that the original of this model saw service in Africa.

The postwar model of the BMW R 75, painted gloss black. This cycle was the "little man's car" in the 1950s. Add saddlebags and a machine-gun mount and this civilian version will be just like the wartime model.

This shows the right side of a heavy Zündapp KS 750 sidecar model. The model was given the tactical symbol of the motorcycle riflemen, the stylized wheel with stylized crossed spokes, and mounted on a diorama. Note the saddlebags on both sides of the sidecar, as well as the mounted MG 34. The MG 42, which later became so renowned, was not used by the motorcycle riflemen.

A left-side view of the heavy Zündapp KS 750, painted dark gray, with various equipment, including the driver's 98 k carbine.

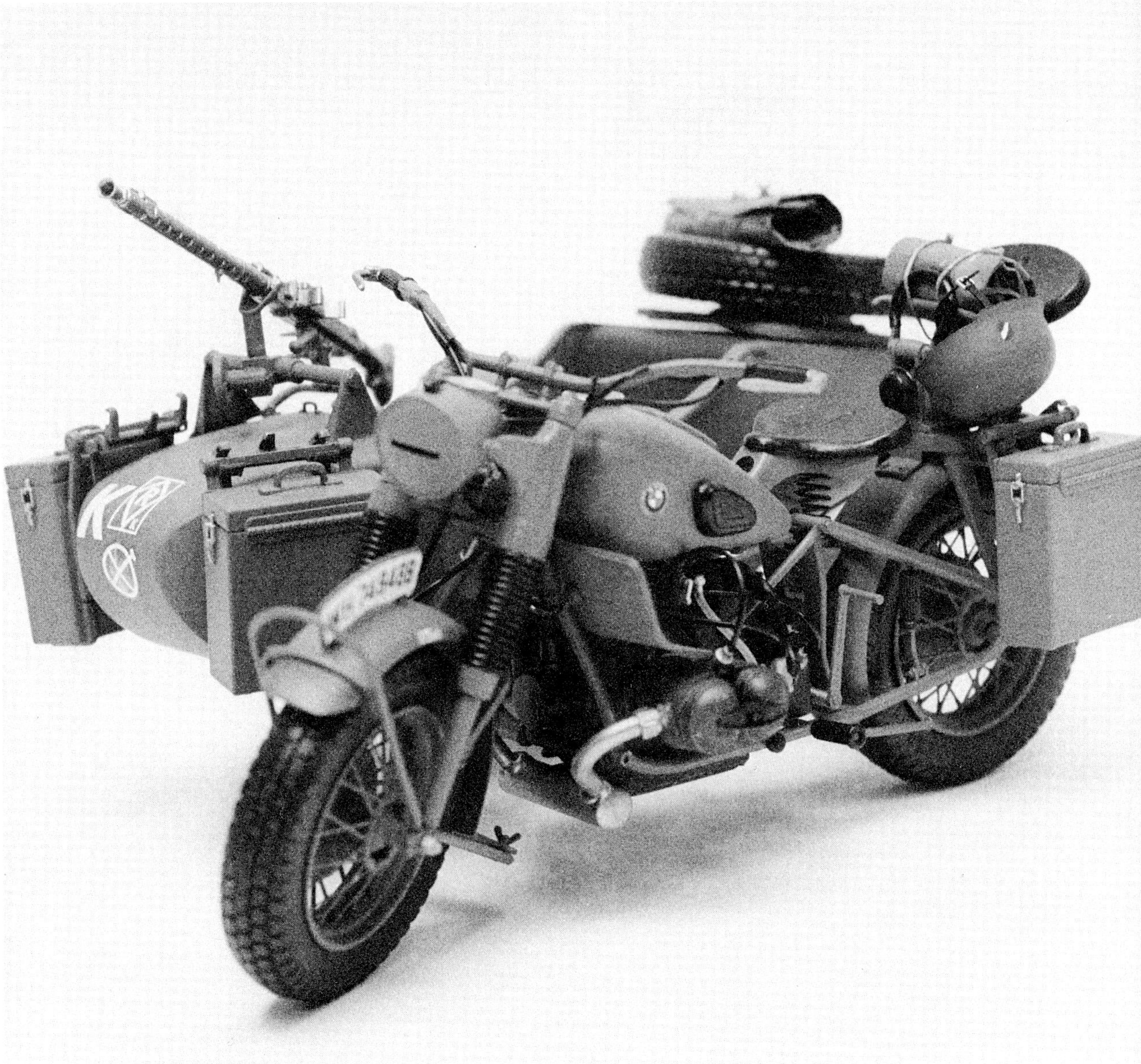

The heavy BMW R 75 motorcycle rifle model, with a mounted MG 34, painted dark gray. The black rubber bellows on the front fork indicate that this model was based on the 1942-43 machine.

The personal equipment of a motorcycle messenger. It included not only cooking vessels and field flask, but also a light Panzerfaust. The ESCI kits feature a wealth of equipment.

For the Collector
Models of Military Motorcycles

In the world of model building, several of the most interesting motorcycles have been put on the market in 1:9 scale over the years. For those who appreciate these historical models, there are thus not only kits of German motorcycles available. In all, the model manufacturer ESCI produces the following kits in the 1:9 scale mentioned above:

BMW R 75 with sidecar
BMW R 75 solo
Zündapp KS 750 with sidecar
Zündapp KS 750 solo
Harley-Davidson WLA 45 solo
Triumph

The kits include a variety of the motorcyclist's personal equipment and various accessories. Detailed construction features in the area of the front fork, the shifting rods for road and off-road gears, the separate drive for the sidecar, etc., guarantee an excellent insight into the construction and mechanism, particularly those of the German sidecar motorcycles. The machines can also be fitted optionally with the so-called "tropical air filter" or with foot-rest heating for winter use.The BMW motorcycles include a spring-mounted front fork with folded rubber bellows such as were used on the originals from the 1942-43 model year on. The headlight covers are also very well made. The saddlebags on the cycle and on both sides of the sidecar are removable. The sidecar can also be built optionally with or without a machine gun and its mount.

As already mentioned, the BMW and Zündapp kits are also available as solo machines. In actual fact, though, both types were put into service exclusively with sidecars. As solo machines, these models actually look "amputated", since the attachment for the driveshaft of the sidecar, to be attached to the right side, is present on the rear axle, while the sidecar itself is missing from the model. Nevertheless, these two German solo motorcycles are also shown here.

No less interesting to look at are the two Harley-Davidson WLA 45 models and the Triumph. These kits also include various individual components and many accessories. In the area of the typical Harley foot-rest boards are several shift levers. The gun holster attached to the front fork holds a carbine. On the other hand, the Triumph, with its tubular frame and big spoked wheels makes a somewhat fragile appearance.

The conclusion of this model show consists of the German BMW R 75 sidecar version in civilian form. After 1945 it was nicknamed the War Elephant. At this time, and until well after 1950, it was the vehicle of the little man. Today these rarities are uncommon and appreciated when seen on our roads. If driven at all, they are driven by their owners only in ideal weather conditions.

Acknowledgements

The assembly of over 250 documentary photographs 47 years after the war ended would not have been possible for me without much help. Friends, acquaintances, relatives, colleagues and strangers have kindly helped to achieve this goal. Whether archivists in libraries who offered me their support or staff members of daily newspapers who kindly published my advertisements for usable photos, my thanks go out to all of them.

Photos and documents were made available by the following individuals and institutions: Photo Archives of the Preussischer Kulturbesitz, BMW AG, Karl Heinz Denzler, Eugen Dürr, Gerhard Elser, Reinhard Frank, Henry Hoppe, Gerhard Kesenhagen, Johanna Klattkowski, Dr. Hans Kohler, Werner Kritter, Munin Verlag, NSU GmbH, Konrad Oberhardt, Horst Scheibert, Joachim Schwaar, Elisabet Serwatzki, Leonhard Spohrer, Hans Sievers and others.

My special thanks go to Dr. Hans Kohler of Neckarsulm. Dr. Kohler assisted me with countless bits of advice during my year-long search for photos, although to this day we have never met face to face. I regard his helpfulness as worthy of special recognition.

I would be very happy if this support would continue to be offered, as I am thinking in terms of an expansion of this book if appropriate photographic material justifies it. Surely numerous photographs of motorcycles and their drivers are "slumbering" in many private photo albums and are worthy of being published.

Photo Credits:
Panzergrenadiere, Kradschützen und Panzeraufklärer by Horst Scheibert, Podzun-Pallas-Verlag, Friedberg, Hessen.
Motorrad Classic, No. 2, 1993.
BMW – Eine deutsche Geschichte, R. Piper GmbH & Co. KG, Munich.
Deutsche Panzergrenadiere, Verlag E. S. Mittler & Sohn GmbH, Herford.
Lastkraftwagen der Wehrmacht by Reinhard Frank, Podzun-Pallas-Verlag.